WITHDRAWN

Scientists at Work

Archaeologists

Rose Inserra

Smart Apple Media

HUNTINGTON CITY-TOWNSHIP
PUBLIC LIBRARY
200 W. Market Street
Huntington IN 46750

This edition first published in 2005 in the United States of America by Smart Apple Media.
Reprinted 2005

All rights reserved. No part of this book may be reproduced in any form or by any means
without written permission from the publisher.

Smart Apple Media
1980 Lookout Drive
North Mankato
Minnesota 56003

Library of Congress Cataloging-in-Publication Data

Inserra, Rose.
  Archaeologists / by Rose Inserra.
  p. cm. — (Scientists at work)
  Includes index.
  ISBN 1-58340-544-5 (alk. paper)
  1. Archaeologists—Juvenile literature. 2. Archaeology—Juvenile literature. 3. Excavations
(Archaeology—Juvenile literature. [1. Archaeologists. 2. Archaeology—Vocational guidance.
3. Vocational guidance.] I. Title. II. Scientists at work (Smart Apple Media)

  CC107.I57 2004
  930.1'092—dc22   2003070430

First Edition
9 8 7 6 5 4 3 2 1

First published in 2004 by
MACMILLAN EDUCATION AUSTRALIA PTY LTD
627 Chapel Street, South Yarra, Australia, 3141

Associated companies and representatives throughout the world.

Copyright © Rose Inserra 2004

Edited by Sally Woollett
Text and cover design by The Modern Art Production Group
Page layout by Raul Diche
Illustrations by Alan Laver, Shelly Communications Pty Ltd and Pat Kermode, Purple Rabbit Productions
Photo research by Jesmondene Senbergs
Printed in China

Acknowledgements

The author and the publisher are grateful to the following for permission to reproduce copyright material:

Cover photograph: Archaeologist with artifacts, courtesy of Corbis.

Associated Press/English Heritage, p. 4; Beverly Chiarulli;, pp. 22, 23; Corbis, pp. 5, 8 (bottom), 9 (bottom), 11, 13,
15 (top left), 20 (bottom), 26, 27, 28; Getty Images, pp. 6, 9 (top); Michelle Glynn, p. 21; Great Southern Stock, p. 15
(middle right); Griffith Institute, Oxford, p. 8 (top); Image Library, p. 14 (bottom left); John Walmsley Education,
p. 30; PENNDOT and FHWA, pp. 24, 25; Photodisc, pp. 15 (bottom right), 19; Photolibrary.com/Super Stock, p. 12;
Science Museum of Minnesota, p. 16 (all); Simon Fraser/Science Photo Library, p. 15 (bottom left); Pascal
Goetgheluck/Science Photo Library, p. 14 (top right); NASA/Science Photo Library, p. 15 (center left); Sam Ogden/
Science Photo Library, p. 15 (top right); Alexis Rosenfield/Science Photo Library, p. 20 (top); Jeremy Smith, p. 21;
The Ancient Art & Architecture Collection, p. 7.

Author acknowledgements

Many thanks to Beverly Chiarulli, Indiana University of Pennsylvania, for kindly agreeing to be interviewed for this
book. Many thanks also to the sponsors of the Philipsburg Tannery project – PENNDOT and the Federal Highway
Administration – and Scott Shaffer of PENNDOT and Scott Emory of A.D. Marble and Company for their assistance
with information on the Philipsburg Tannery excavation.

While every care has been taken to trace and acknowledge copyright, the publisher tenders their apologies for any
accidental infringement where copyright has proved untraceable. Where the attempt has been unsuccessful, the
publisher welcomes information that would redress the situation.

Please note

At the time of printing, the Internet addresses appearing in this book were correct. Owing to the dynamic nature of
the Internet, however, we cannot guarantee that all these addresses will remain correct.

Contents

Glossary words

When you see a word printed in **bold**, you can look up its meaning in the glossary on page 31.

What is an archaeologist?

An archaeologist is a scientist who studies the lives of people in the past by finding remains and digging up certain areas, or sites. These sites may contain artifacts, which are items made or used by people in the past. Tools, pots, and jewelry are all examples of artifacts.

Many archaeologists have special skills in digging up sites. They are called field archaeologists. These scientists **survey** a particular area in the world or a particular past **culture**. They do this by visiting these areas and digging for artifacts. This is called a dig.

Archaeologists use equipment before, during, and after a dig. Before starting a dig, they survey the area of interest, and they may take photographs and use instruments such as metal detectors. During the dig, archaeologists use tools such as picks and shovels, and then analyze the data after the dig using computers.

Scientists
working together

Archaeologists often work with other scientists. Biologists and geologists help archaeologists gather information from soil samples and vegetation. Forensic scientists are usually asked for help with human body parts from crime scenes. Physicists and chemists use various methods to find out information such as the age of an object. Palaeontologists study remains of fossils and bones, such as those from dinosaurs and human **ancestors**.

This archaeologist is carefully digging around the tusk of a mammoth that lived during the Ice Age.

4

The role of archaeologists

Archaeologists play an important part in the community. They spend time looking for information from artifacts or from the natural environment. This helps us to understand our ancestors and how they lived, as well as the environment that they lived in.

Features such as tombs, cities, pyramids, temples, and buildings give us information about how people used to build and what materials they used. Archaeologists gather information about past cultures from artifacts such as weapons, tools, jewelry and art. Ecofacts are environmental remains (such as plant remains). Environmental remains such as bones, skeletons, grain, charcoal, sand, shells, and pollen from plants are examples of ecofacts. Ecofacts can help us understand the changes in the environment since ancient times.

Museum archaeologists **conserve** artifacts for display in museums so that the public can learn about archaeology. Archaeologists train and teach archaeology students in colleges.

Fact Box

Archaeologist Stuart Piggot called archaeology "the science of rubbish" because it involves digging up things that people in the past threw out. The word "archaeology" comes from the Greek language and means "the study of that which is ancient."

These interesting pottery artifacts belonged to people who lived a long time ago.

Archaeology in the past

Archaeology has only been a formal science for the past few hundred years. Before this, people doing digs did not work to a method or keep proper records of artifacts they found.

Fact Box

Sir William Flinders Petrie (1852–1942) was the earliest modern archaeologist. Petrie developed an organized system of digging, and recording everything in **chronological** order.

The Rosetta Stone

The Rosetta Stone code

Napoleon Bonaparte was a leader of the French army in the late 1700s. In 1798, when he invaded Egypt, he took scientists, surveyors, and engineers to record what he found on his expeditions. In 1799, near the town of Rosetta in northern Egypt, Napoleon's soldiers found a large slab of rock with writing on it, the Rosetta Stone. The text was written in three languages:

- Egyptian hieroglyphs, an ancient form of picture writing
- demotic Egyptian, a later form of Egyptian writing
- Greek

In 1822, a young Frenchman, Jean François Champollion, recognized a word on the Rosetta Stone. Eventually, archaeologists could understand all of the ancient Egyptian hieroglyphs by comparing it with the same text in the other two languages.

Key events in archaeology	1799 Rosetta Stone is found in Egypt.	1911 Hiram Bingham finds the city of Machu Picchu in Peru.	1961 Neolithic site of Çatalhöyük in Turkey is excavated.
1763 Ruins of the city of Pompeii are discovered in Italy.	1870 Heinrich Schliemann begins excavation of the city of Troy in Turkey.	1922 Howard Carter discovers King Tutankhamen's tomb in Egypt.	

Progress in archaeology

During the 1800s there were many important archaeological discoveries. Most discoveries were made by people with little experience in archaeology and so methods used to dig up sites were very basic. Sometimes damage was done to things that were found.

Digging up Troy

Heinrich Schliemann was one of the first archaeologists. He was determined to find the lost city of Troy, which he had read about in an ancient poem, written by Homer, called *The Iliad*. He used Homer's description of the landscape in the poem to help him find the site. In 1870, he began digging a mound in Hissarlik in western Turkey.

Schliemann found out that there was not just a single city of Troy on the site, but several cities built up in layers over time. He was so eager to reach the oldest layer, which he thought was the Troy in *The Iliad*, that he did not record the upper layers. The problem was that these upper layers were the Troy he was looking for, not the lower ones. Much of the evidence he wanted was destroyed.

Sophia Schliemann wore the treasures that her husband discovered.

Fact Box

How did Schliemann know that he had missed the city of Troy described in *The Iliad*? In 1873, when he explored some of the upper layers of Troy, he found 250 gold objects in the city he had dug right through.

1974
Clay warriors are found in underground pits near an Emperor's tomb in China.

1991
Mummy of Ötzi the Iceman is discovered in the Italian mountains.

2000
Philipsburg Tannery excavated in Pennsylvania.

1985
Shipwreck of the *Titanic* is located underwater in the Atlantic Ocean.

1994
Alexandria Harbor in Egypt is explored underwater. Stones from the Pharos lighthouse are found.

Important discoveries

Many important discoveries have helped archaeologists learn more about life in the past.

King Tut's tomb

Archaeologist Howard Carter spent 20 years digging in the Valley of the Kings in Egypt. In 1922, he found a doorway shut with an ancient royal seal. This meant that he was the first to pass through the doorway for over 3,000 years. He made a small hole to inspect the unopened burial chamber. What he saw amazed him.

Carter had found the royal tomb of Tutankhamen, a **pharaoh** who died in 1327 B.C. The chamber contained all the things that the king would need for his afterlife, including a golden throne, jewelry, utensils, and weapons. The most famous discovery was the **sarcophagus**, in which the pharaoh's **mummy** lay. There were three coffins, one inside the other. The outer two coffins were made of gilded wood, and the innermost coffin and death mask were made of solid gold.

This is King Tutankhamen's golden face mask.

The ruins of Machu Picchu are high in the mountains.

Machu Picchu

In 1911, archaeologist Hiram Bingham came across the city of Machu Picchu, a fortress city in the Andes mountains in Peru. He had no idea that he had stumbled on an ancient native South American Indian (Inca) site.

Some historians believe that the city was a sacred site for worship. Others believe that it may have been a hiding place from the Spanish invaders, who arrived in 1532.

The Emperor's army

In 1974, farmers digging a well at Mount Li in China stumbled across a series of huge pits. The pits contained about 7,000 clay warriors in full armor. This was the burial site of China's first emperor, Ch'in Shi-huang-ti, who ruled from 221 to 210 B.C. and was responsible for building the Great Wall of China.

The clay warriors are life size, and are believed to be copies of his real army. No two warriors look the same. There are kneeling archers, standing archers, cavalry with saddled horses, charioteers, and infantry, as well as officers, wearing uniform of their rank.

Known as the "Emperor's army," these clay warriors were discovered in China.

Pompeii

On August 24 in A.D. 79, when the volcano Vesuvius violently erupted, the city of Pompeii in southern Italy was destroyed, buried under ash. When Vesuvius erupted it sent ash and **lava** into the air and about 2,000 people died. They were smothered in the ash and buried.

The city was rediscovered in 1637 and **excavation** of the site began in 1738. Artifacts and treasures were stolen and features were damaged as wealthy people took artifacts for collection. Today, the ruins of the city are still being excavated. Stores, houses, roads, gateways, temples, brightly colored wall paintings, as well as thousands of artifacts, can be seen.

These are the remains of buildings that were buried in ash when the volcano Mount Vesuvius erupted in Pompeii.

ACCIDENT OR MURDER? SECRETS FROM THE ICEMAN'S ICY TOMB

When a body was found near the border between Austria and Italy in September 1991, the police began a hunt for missing tourists. Who would have believed that the frozen body belonged to a man in his forties who lived in the area 5,300 years ago?

The Iceman was found near the border of Austria and Italy.

New tests have revealed some amazing facts that may finally answer the question of how he died.

The body, known as Ötzi the Iceman, was perfectly **preserved** under the ice, but rescuers thought they were collecting a recent body, so they did not preserve the body correctly. He was found wearing leather shoes, a coat of leather and goat fur, and a cap made out of brown bear fur. He carried tools with him such as a copper axe, a stone dagger, a bow, a wood-framed backpack, a leather pouch for arrows, and some fire-lighting gear. He also had an arrow repair kit in a small leather bag. That told archaeologists that he was well prepared and a regular traveler. So what caused him to die? Was it an accident or murder?

The Iceman's 5,000-year-old body is in excellent condition.

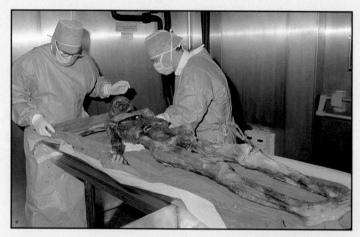

Using X-rays and a special medical scan, scientists saw what appeared to be rib fractures. They suggested that the Iceman may have been a shepherd or hunter who died from a fall in the mountains. He may also have been fleeing from danger. One thing they were almost sure about was that the cause of death was exposure to cold. The Iceman may have been caught in a storm.

In 1998, when Ötzi was moved to a specially built museum in Bolzano, Italy, more detailed tests were done. A special refrigerated chamber was built to keep the Iceman in the same condition in which he was found. Forensic scientists reconstructed Ötzi's face from his skull by using special medical scan data. At last the world knew what the Iceman had looked like!

From tooth and bone samples, Ötzi was found to be from the Italian side of the border. **Botanists** looked at the contents of his stomach to work out his last meal, which was bread made from grains used at the time he lived, and meat. Pollen from the hop hornbeam tree was also found on the body. This pollen came from a warmer valley climate. The Iceman had eaten his last meal down in the valley, where it was warmer, only about eight hours before he died.

In June 2001, scientists X-rayed the body again and found a strange object near the shoulder. They had discovered a stone arrowhead stuck in Ötzi's shoulder — death by murder! An **autopsy** now needs to be done on the body to pull out the arrowhead before we will know what took place in the final hours before the Iceman's death.

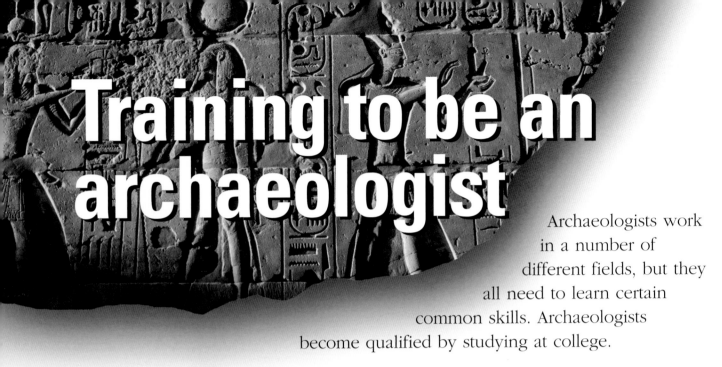

Training to be an archaeologist

Archaeologists work in a number of different fields, but they all need to learn certain common skills. Archaeologists become qualified by studying at college.

Fact Box

A bachelor's degree takes four years to complete.

At school

Archaeology is both a science and an art, so high school students who want to become archaeologists need to study subjects such as history, math, and science. Being good at languages is also helpful because archaeologists may travel to different countries to work.

Subjects archaeologists use are:

- math called statistics to examine the data from sites
- biology to identify the bone, plant, and shell material they excavate
- history to build a picture of how people lived in the past
- anthropology, the study of human culture and biology, to help them understand the relationships between people
- ancient languages such as Latin or symbols such as Egyptian hieroglyphs to help them understand ancient writing

Archaeologists must train to do field work.

A college degree

After finishing high school, people who want to become archaeologists study a Bachelor of Science or a Bachelor of Arts degree at college. They also study anthropology, a history subject related to archaeology, and train to do field work.

Farther study

Archaeology students who have completed their bachelor's degree can do more study, called graduate study. Students who have completed graduate studies can become crew supervisors or principal investigators on archaeological projects, and some can teach at colleges. Graduate studies can take many years to complete.

After their final year of college, most students begin working as professional archaeologists.

At work

Most archaeologists will have had some practical experience of excavation while completing their degrees. Archaeologists who have completed their degrees continue to learn more about their work throughout their careers. Many do field work in different places around the world. These experiences add to their knowledge of archaeology.

On-the-job training

Like anyone in a skilled profession, archaeologists keep on learning more about their subject. They attend seminars and conferences, and read books and journals. Archaeological science is developing all the time and archaeologists have to keep up to date with the latest findings.

Archaeologists are always learning!

These archaeologists are working on an excavation in Israel.

Tools and instruments

Archaeologists use many different tools and instruments to do their work. They use tools and instruments in the field, in the laboratory, and in the office.

Survey tools

Archaeologists may walk around an area looking for above-ground evidence. This could be pits, mounds, ditches, or structures. They may use paper and pencil to make a sketch of the site, and mark out and map the site using a compass and tape.

Magnetometer

Magnetometers

Magnetometers measure disturbances in a special force around the Earth called a magnetic field. The disturbances are caused by different levels in the ground, particularly hollow spaces. This instrument is used to show walls, pits, and ditches, so that digging can be carried out without unnecessary damage.

Excavating tools

To conduct an excavation, archaeologists use picks, shovels, **trowels**, and buckets for digging. They use brushes, sieves, and small tools for cleaning, and measuring instruments for recording and drawing the site. Sometimes bulldozers are used.

Shovel

Radar

Radar stands for **RA**dio **D**etection **A**nd **R**anging. It is a system of sending radio waves, which bounce back when they hit objects and show on a screen what the objects look like. Ground radar sends out waves of radiation so that buried river channels, crypts, wells, and tunnels can be located. It is used in built-up areas because it does not interfere with metals or electricity.

Resistivity meters

Resistivity meters are used to find out information about conditions underground. A site may contain buried walls, stony surfaces, ditches, or high moisture. To make measurements, the probe of the resistivity meter is inserted into different parts of the ground around the site.

Metal detector

Metal detectors

Metal detectors are sometimes used on sites to detect metals underneath the ground.

Aerial photograph

Photographs

Aerial photographs are used to locate new sites without disturbing them and can show existing sites with the natural landscape around them. Differences in ground levels, shades, colors, and crop marks can all suggest buried sites.

Global positioning system

Satellites

The global positioning system (GPS) is an accurate way to locate any site from anywhere in the world. It is a system that uses satellites to locate the position of objects on Earth to within a few feet. This allows archaeologists to carry out detailed searches. Two receivers on the ground pick up the signals sent by satellites and then the data is recorded on a computer.

Robot with camera

Robots

TV cameras are sometimes fitted to small robots. These robots can enter small enclosed spaces to record information.

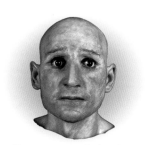
Reconstructed clay face

Clay

Reconstructing a face using a skull can show how a person looked when they were alive. To do this, medical artists and archaeologists apply layers of special clay to the skull and fill it in to look like a normal face.

X-rays

X-ray machines are used to see what is under the rusty outer layer of metal objects before conservation takes place. The machine shows details that cannot be seen by the naked eye. X-ray machines and medical scanners have also been used to examine mummies. They give clear detail of what is inside the bodies so that archaeologists can handle the mummy and not disturb its contents.

Computer

Computers

Computers are used to sort information such as three-dimensional images when reconstructing a skull or site plan. Computers can be used for on-site recording of structures and artifacts.

Back   Forward   Stop   Refresh   Home   AutoFill   Print   History   Favorites   Add   Search   Larger

Address: @   〉go

Visit Çatalhöyük, the oldest town in history!

Welcome to the site of Çatalhöyük, 37 miles (60 km) southeast of Konya in Turkey. The site is easily reached by car and you can visit at any time of the year. Snowfalls are expected in the winter months, so please be prepared.

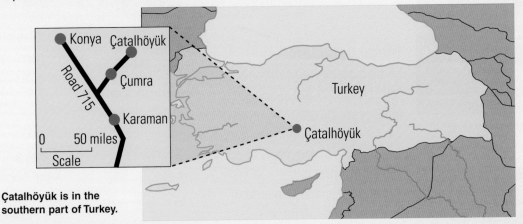

Çatalhöyük is in the southern part of Turkey.

History of Çatalhöyük

The **Neolithic** town of Çatalhöyük was first excavated by archaeologist James Mellaart between 1961 and 1965. It was the oldest town ever discovered, dated at 6250 B.C., as well as the largest, with a population of 5,000 at one time.

Çatalhöyük was built up over time in mounds, created by 7,000 years of people living there, just building on top of each other, layer upon layer.

Excavated mounds at Çatalhöyük show the many layers of houses and buildings built upon each other since Neolithic times.

Internet zone

Address: @   › go

Amazing finds

Over 40 rooms in the settlement are decorated with bull skulls made from plaster and bull horns. Other decorations featuring the bull include bull shrines, pillars with horns, and wall paintings.

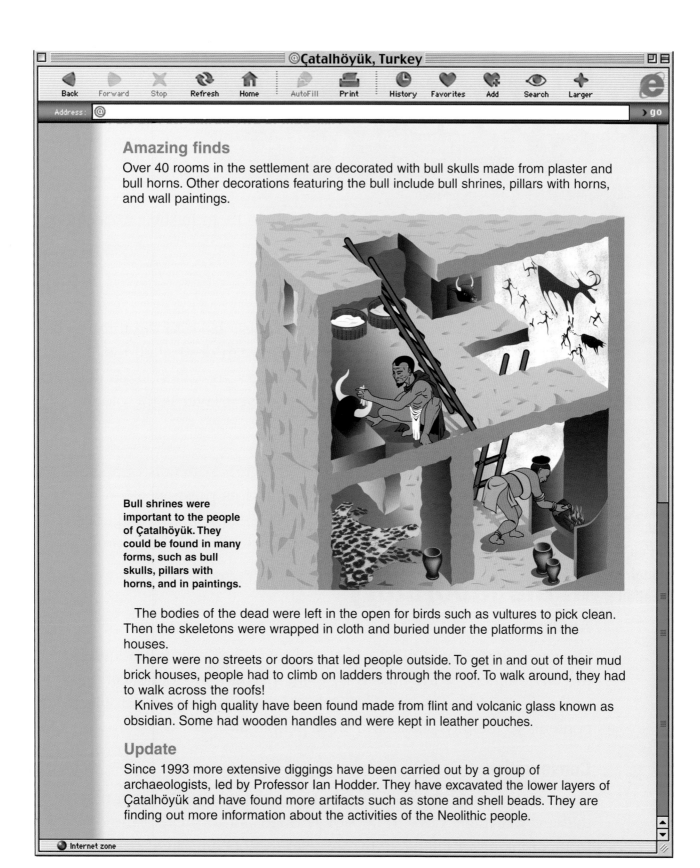

Bull shrines were important to the people of Çatalhöyük. They could be found in many forms, such as bull skulls, pillars with horns, and in paintings.

The bodies of the dead were left in the open for birds such as vultures to pick clean. Then the skeletons were wrapped in cloth and buried under the platforms in the houses.

There were no streets or doors that led people outside. To get in and out of their mud brick houses, people had to climb on ladders through the roof. To walk around, they had to walk across the roofs!

Knives of high quality have been found made from flint and volcanic glass known as obsidian. Some had wooden handles and were kept in leather pouches.

Update

Since 1993 more extensive diggings have been carried out by a group of archaeologists, led by Professor Ian Hodder. They have excavated the lower layers of Çatalhöyük and have found more artifacts such as stone and shell beads. They are finding out more information about the activities of the Neolithic people.

Internet zone

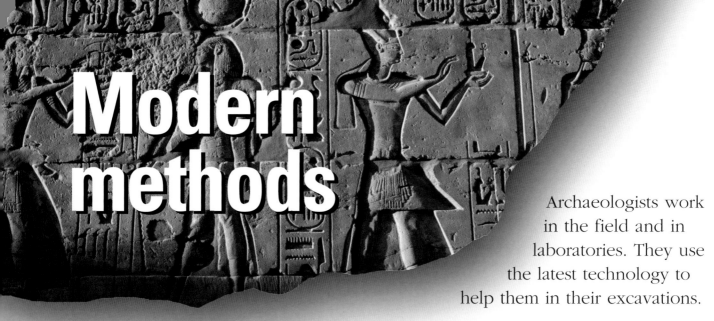

Modern methods

Archaeologists work in the field and in laboratories. They use the latest technology to help them in their excavations.

In the field

Digging through layers

Excavating a site can destroy it. Archaeologists have to dig through the upper layers to get to the ones below. This can destroy all the evidence in the excavated ground. The layers are called strata and they show different times of occupation. The lowest layer is the oldest.

Observing and recording

Archaeologists have to look carefully at the tiniest details of a site. Every artifact has to be labeled, bagged, and its position recorded on a plan of the site. Archaeologists need to use maps, plans, diagrams, databases, and computer-generated models to record the information.

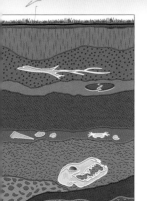

Layers in an archaeological dig are called strata.

In the laboratory

Analysis

Objects from the field need to be analyzed. One way to understand the environment of the time is by using palynology, identification of pollen grains found on sites. This method can be used for stomach contents to identify plants and what people ate.

Conservation

Conservation is extremely important in archaeology. Wooden objects that are wet might have to be slowly dried out to prevent the object from shrinking or falling apart. Sometimes pots are glued back together to see what they looked like.

Relative and absolute dating

The two types of dating are relative and absolute. Relative dates tell us that one thing is older than another. Absolute dates are dates that can be expressed in actual years or periods of time.

Seriation

One method of working out relative dating is seriation. As artifacts are excavated, they are kept in the order in which they are excavated, which is youngest to oldest. When an archaeologist finds the same type of artifact at another part of the site, he or she can compare it with the ordered artifacts to estimate its age. This is mainly used for pottery.

Dendrochronology

This is one of the oldest ways of working out an absolute date. When trees grow, they produce a circular pattern in their wood, called a growth ring. Trees produce one new ring each year, and the thickness of each ring depends on the climate. Trees that grow in the same area are affected in the same way by the climate conditions, so they show similar patterns of rings. Wooden objects and fossilized trees can be dated by comparing their ring patterns to those of trees of a known age.

Radiocarbon dating

Radiocarbon dating is a dating technique used in the laboratory. A special type of carbon that is **radioactive** exists in all living things. This carbon in our bodies decays over time. Archaeologists can measure the amount of carbon left in something that was once living and then work out how much time has passed in order for this amount of decay to have happened. This method is useful for dating bone and also food items such as plant matter and shellfish.

Tree rings can be used to work out the age of wooden objects.

Working on location

Archaeologists work in different parts of the world depending on their projects. Some digs will take them to locations such as the Middle East, where they may have to live with a harsh climate, uncomfortable living conditions, and sometimes political problems. Some archaeologists risk danger when diving to underwater sites.

Fact Box

In 1985, a famous underwater shipwreck, the *Titanic*, was found. The enormous ocean liner sank after it collided with an iceberg. Using special scanners and a **submersible** with video cameras, the *Titanic* was found lying on the seabed in two pieces.

Divers record the measurements of artifacts they recover.

The Pharos lighthouse

In 1994, French marine archaeologists searched the bottom of the Mediterranean Sea for artifacts from the ancient city of Alexandria in Egypt. They found remains of palaces, statues, sphinxes, and blocks of stone from the tallest building at the time, the Pharos lighthouse. The lighthouse was built in 280 B.C. and collapsed in the water after an earthquake in the 1300s.

The latest technology was used to recover all the lighthouse remains. Very detailed maps had to be charted with GPS because of the huge size of the blocks, which were piled up on top of each other. Architects and engineers were on site to offer advice. Divers used air-filled parachute-shaped balloons to lift the large stones from the seabed.

Underwater excavation has many dangers. Divers run the risk of running low on air or getting caught in nets or snares. An unstable seabed, stormy weather conditions, and the risk of large artifacts collapsing can cause major injuries.

Many treasures have been found under the sea.

Urgent excavations

When the Syrian government decided to build a dam in the upper Euphrates River, it meant that important archaeological sites would be flooded and destroyed. The ancient Assyrian city of **Tell** Ahmar was to be among them. Since 1988, the University of Melbourne, Australia, has sent archaeologists and students to dig at the site, hoping to learn as much as possible about the city's architecture and artifacts before it was destroyed.

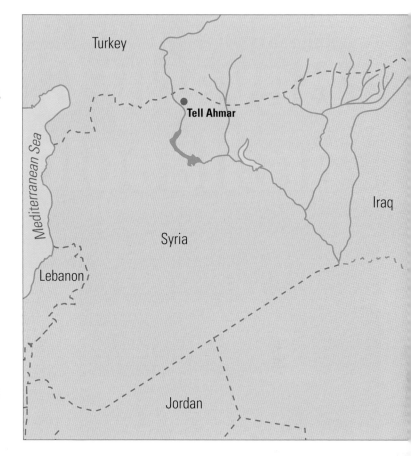

The archaeologists wanted to answer some questions. What was the importance of this city, how did people live, and who were the original people before the city was taken over by the Assyrians? All these questions needed to be answered before the dam was to be completed in 1997. However, archaeologists faced problems with the site. Recent plowing of fields by farmers meant that the shape of the city wall could no longer be seen. A village was now on the actual area of the site, so work had to progress at a slower pace.

Tell Ahmar is an excavated city in Syria, a country in the Middle East.

In hot countries such as Syria, climate can be a problem. Shade and drinking water need to be available at all times. Insects, reptiles, and other dangerous creatures are also a hazard. Accidents can happen more easily because the territory is unfamiliar. Archaeologists understand the dangers of field work in countries such as Syria, and by carefully planning ahead they can avoid trouble. The information they collect will help us to understand our past, before all the evidence is destroyed.

Many pottery artifacts have been found at Tell Ahmar.

Beverly Chiarulli, archaeologist

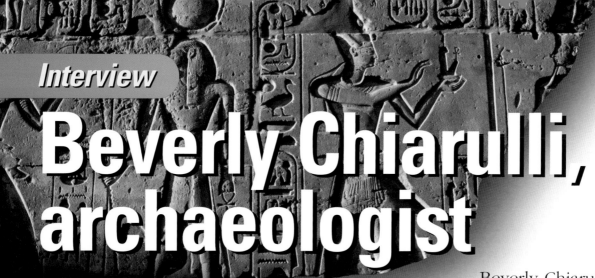

Beverly Chiarulli is an Assistant Professor in the Anthropology Department and Director of Archaeological Services at Indiana University of Pennsylvania.

What does your job involve?

We have just completed a large data recovery project on one historic site and three **prehistoric** sites south of the campus. I also spend a lot of my time writing proposals, and speaking to K–12 school students and local groups about archaeology. The other half of my job is teaching in the Anthropology Department.

Who else is involved in your projects?

Most commonly, a geomorphologist, who studies landforms, erosion, and soil deposits. A historic archaeologist conducts historic background research. Sometimes a geographer is involved.

What do you like most about your job?

I like the fact that every day is different and that we always have new projects to work on. I like putting together the pieces of information we discover into a pattern that tells us about the past. I like working with students and seeing them grow and learn during the four years they are at college.

What are the dangers in your job?

The main dangers are car accidents. You do have to watch out for the occasional snake or scorpion, but these rarely cause serious problems. Insects, like mosquitoes, are more of a problem. You need to be aware of diseases in the areas you work and take appropriate precautions like vaccines. Sunburn can be a problem. You should know basic first aid.

What was your most exciting archaeological project?

One of the most exciting was the very first project I worked on at the University of Illinois field school at Cahokia Mounds, Illinois. We excavated in some large borrow pits that the site's inhabitants had excavated for soil. The soil was used to construct large platform mounds. The borrow pits were then filled with layers of trash that told us a lot about life at the site.

The other site that I found most exciting was Cerros, in northern Belize, where I did my **dissertation** research. I worked there for four years and in one area of the site excavated part of the earliest village area. I also excavated what turned out to be one of three ball courts. These are three of the earliest ball courts in the Maya lowlands and date to around A.D. 100.

What are some exciting developments in archaeology?

I think some of the advances in technology are very exciting. Ground-penetrating radar, magnetometers, and resistivity can change the way we approach investigations.

What qualities do you need to become an archaeologist?

You need to be patient, able to work outdoors in all kinds of weather, interested in everything, and not bothered by a little dirt.

What advice would you give people who are interested in archaeology as a career?

Be interested in everything. Get as much experience as you can to see if archaeology is what you really like.

Beverly Chiarulli working at a site in Pennsylvania.

Philipsburg Tannery, Pennsylvania

Read this dig report to find out more about the work of a volunteer who helped to excavate a site that was once a tannery.

Site: Philipsburg Tannery site, Pennsylvania (1870–1903)

Date of excavation: 2000–2001

The project

The excavation of the tannery is taking place before a new highway is built on the location. A tannery is a factory where hides of animals are cleaned, treated, and processed into leather goods. In the last century tanneries manufactured goods such as belts, shoes, boots, harnesses for horses, and items of clothing. I had no idea the tanning process was such complicated and hard work. It took about 8 to 10 months to complete the process and many buildings were used.

First tannery

The first tannery was built in 1870 and was called the Philipsburg Leather Manufacturing Company. This tannery processed about 30,000 hides a year. In 1876, it burned down but was soon rebuilt into a much larger plant. This was called the Moshannon Tannery.

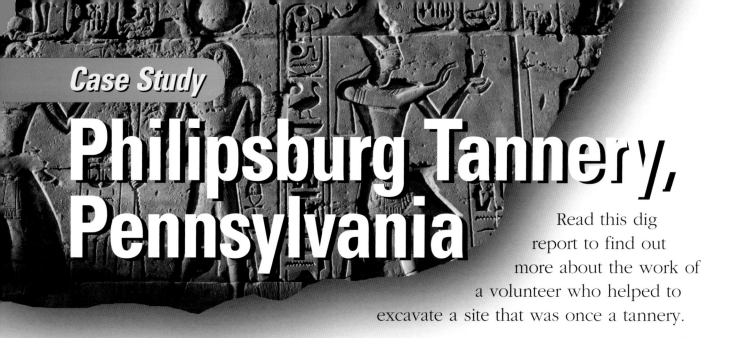

The tannery was excavated before a new highway was built.

Discoveries

At this site, we discovered seven tenement houses where the tannery workers lived, a hide house where machines and vats were used to clean and soften hides, bark sheds where tan bark was stored, and other buildings. The tannery also had a blacksmith's shop, a carpenter's shop, a grease house where oils were extracted from hides, and a beam house where the hair and flesh were stripped from the hides.

Records

From historical records, I found out that the tannery was sold in 1903 to be used as farmland. A few years later, the land was divided into housing lots. What was life like during this time? It was a time when machines were taking the place of work done by hand. Using research and the results of the excavation, I was able to get a clearer picture of the activities that went on at the site.

Structures and artifacts

We found foundations of buildings and remains of tannery vats. It was exciting to find artifacts such as nails, knives, and hooks. Items belonging to tannery workers or those living nearby included buttons, a pipe stem, ceramic plates, and glass bottles.

We found toys, canning jars, and bottles too, but these were from after the tannery was pulled down. They probably belonged to people from the farms or houses that were there later. Archaeologists have to be accurate with time sequence.

I now know so much more about how people worked and lived in this 19th-century industrial site.

Tannery foundations

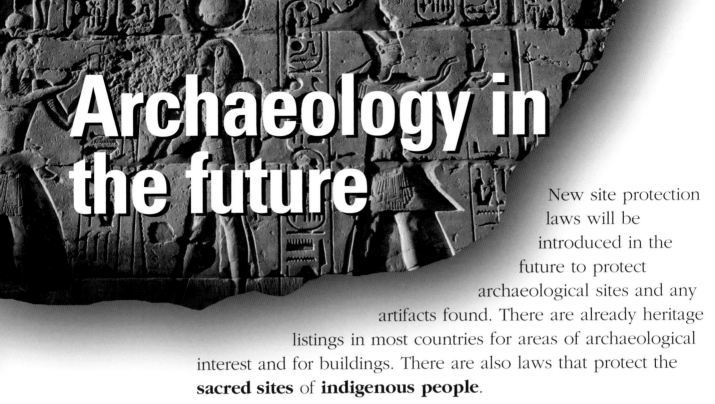

Archaeology in the future

New site protection laws will be introduced in the future to protect archaeological sites and any artifacts found. There are already heritage listings in most countries for areas of archaeological interest and for buildings. There are also laws that protect the **sacred sites** of **indigenous people**.

DNA and molecular archaeology

Archaeologists are now beginning to use a material found in all living things called **d**eoxyribo**n**ucleic **a**cid (DNA). Everybody has different DNA, but some of their DNA is the same as the DNA of their relatives. DNA research can be used in archaeology to trace the relatives of ancient bodies that have been discovered. This method was used to confirm that human remains found in Russia were those of the last **tsar**, Nicholas, and his family. This new area is called molecular archaeology.

Tsar Nicholas of Russia and his family were identified by their DNA.

Computers

Computers are useful today for drawing site plans, reconstructing faces, and using three-dimensional images to give us a full picture of what people or places looked like in the past. Many archaeologists now take laptop computers to their excavations and input data as they dig. Computers will be used more and more in analyzing the data collected from archaeological sites.

Robots

The use of robots will increase for sites that are difficult to get into or do not need to be touched. Some tombs in Italy have been examined without digging into them. A probe is pushed underground and a tiny video camera sends back the picture from inside the tomb. In this way, the site is not disturbed.

Geophysical surveying

Once an area has been located for a dig, aerial photographs are taken. More specific information is provided by GPS and this is likely to increase in archaeology in the future, making it easier to locate sites.

This probe is used for underwater exploration, such as shipwrecks.

A number of tools are used before digging and destroying a site to see what lies beneath the soil. Information is then entered into a computer and a geophysical map is made of the site. In the future, more advances are likely to be made in the surveying area to make these tests quicker. Further remote surveying may be done from the International Space Station.

Fact Box

A tiny robot was sent into a previously unknown narrow shaft of the Great Pyramid of Cheops in Giza in 1994. The robot came up to a blockage, a stone door with copper handles. What was it? Could medical probes one day fit through tiny cracks to see inside?

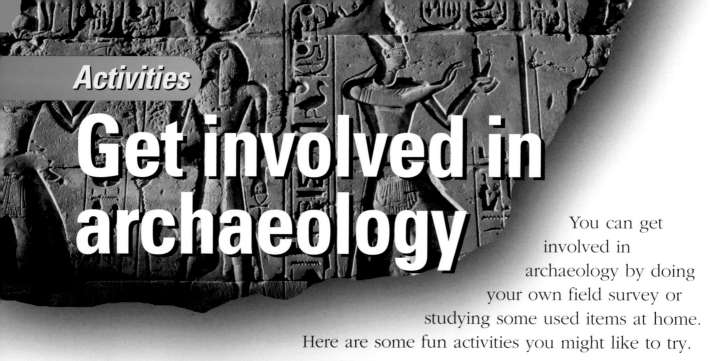

Get involved in archaeology

You can get involved in archaeology by doing your own field survey or studying some used items at home. Here are some fun activities you might like to try.

Garbage study

You will need:

- contents of recycling containers from two different households, e.g. plastic containers, cans, bottles, glass jars, paper products
- gardening gloves

What to do:

1 Wearing your gloves, lay out the contents of each bin separately.
2 Make a list of the contents for each bin.
3 Write down any similarities and differences. Do you eat the same cereal? Does your family drink soy milk or cow's milk? Does this mean that someone in your family is allergic to milk?
4 Make some comments about the type of household. Dog food cans and baby food containers mean that there are a pet and a baby in the family. Lots of tissue boxes means that someone has a cold.
5 Make a site conclusion about the artifacts you found.

Safety

! Some of the items in your recycling bins may be sharp. Wear sturdy gloves to avoid cutting your hands.

Field survey

Go on a field survey where you walk around in an area and use your skills to locate a dig site. Use tools that can help you, such as a metal detector, a map, compass, and digging tools.

Map an archaeological site

You will need:

- pencil and paper
- tape measure
- string
- spade
- wooden or metal object (e.g. an old spoon)

What to do:

1 Look around your back garden and make notes about what the different parts of the garden are used for. There may be a vegetable garden, clothes line, compost heap, or dog house.

2 Take note of vegetation and changes in the ground. Where is it high or low? Where is it dry or damp?

3 Select a part of the garden that you think would make an interesting survey site. (Ask an adult's permission to dig in the garden.)

4 Draw a detailed plan of this area. Use a tape measure to measure out your site, and mark out your site with some string.

5 Write your measurements on your plan and include details of the things you noticed in steps 1 and 2.

6 Dig into your survey site and make notes, on anything you find. Look for changes in the surrounding soil as well as in any objects you find. Are there stains in the ground where the object has broken down?

7 If you do not find anything, bury your old object. Dig it up a year later and see what changes have taken place.

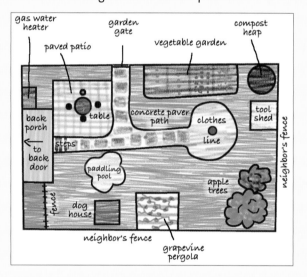

More to do

Get your whole class involved in archaeology!

- Make a time capsule and bury it in the school yard. You will need permission from your teacher. Fill the capsule (this can be a metal box) and label it with the date exactly ten years from now. Place things in it that you are using and remember to dig it up in ten years' time!

- Ask an archaeologist to give a talk to your class.

HUNTINGTON CITY-TOWNSHIP
PUBLIC LIBRARY
200 W. Market Street
Huntington IN 46750

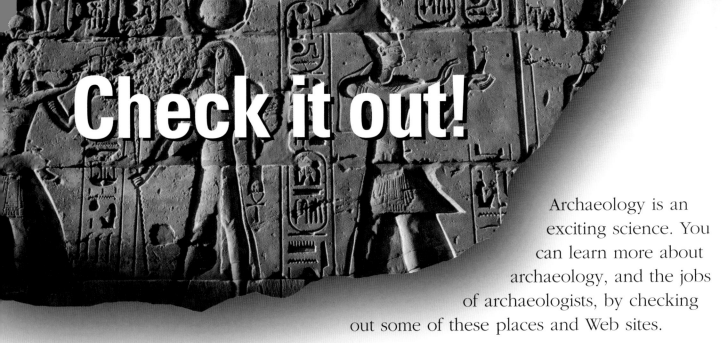

Check it out!

Archaeology is an exciting science. You can learn more about archaeology, and the jobs of archaeologists, by checking out some of these places and Web sites.

Archaeological sites

Lots of archaeological sites are in easy reach and there are often digs happening, like the one at the Philipsburg Tannery. Contact your local historical society or college archaeology school and they will let you know about new digs. Volunteering on an archaeological site is a great way to find out if you would enjoy becoming an archaeologist. Check with museums, local colleges, or on the Internet to find a program you can participate in.

Museums

Most museums, even small local ones, will have an archaeologist on staff who could talk to you about archaeology in your local area. A visit to your local museum might be a good place to start.

You can learn a lot about archaeology in a museum.

Web sites

Association for the Preservation of Virginia Antiquities
http://www.apva.org/
Philipsburg Tannery, Pennsylvania http://www.philipsburgtannery.com/
Southeast Archeological Center (SEAC)
http://www.cr.nps.gov/seac/seac.htm
Ancient Egypt www.ancientegypt.co.uk
Buried Sunken treasures of Alexandria www.pbs.org/wgbh/nova/sunken
Çatalhöyük http://www.catalhuyuk.com

Glossary

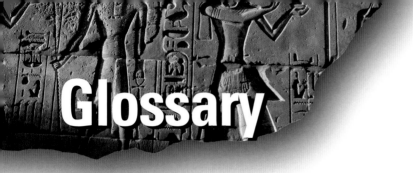

aerial   in the air

ancestors   people who lived before us

autopsy   examination of a body after death to determine the cause (also called a post-mortem)

botanists   scientists who study plants

cesspits   holes dug by people in the past to dump their garbage

chronological   in order of time

conservators   people who conserve things

conserve   prepare an artifact or ecofact to keep it in good condition

culture   customs and traditions of a particular time or people

dissertation   a long essay written by someone doing graduate study to obtain a PhD or doctorate

excavation   the process of digging an archaeological site

heritage   something preserved and passed on from one generation to another, such as a tradition or a building

indigenous people   the original people to settle in a country

lava   hot liquid rock from deep within the Earth

mummy   a preserved body

Neolithic   a period of time also known as the New Stone Age. This tells us that artifacts were made from polished stone.

pharaoh   an ancient Egyptian king

prehistoric   before people developed writing

preserved   kept in good condition and free from decay

radioactive   giving off radiation (a form of energy)

sacred sites   places that have a special meaning

sarcophagus   a coffin

submersible   a small underwater vessel that is launched from a ship

survey   look at a site and make maps and plans of it

tell   the name given in the Middle East to the hills that have been created by people living in the one place for a very long time

trowels   digging tools with short handles

tsar   a name once used for the rulers of Russia

working class   people who had jobs that involved manual labor

Index